MW01599526

likely
stories

OTHER BOOKS BY
PAMELA PORTER

Defending Darkness
(Ronsdale Press, 2016)

House Made of Rain
(Ronsdale Press, 2014)

Late Moon (Ronsdale Press, 2013)

No Ordinary Place
(Ronsdale Press, 2012)

I'll Be Watching
(Groundwood Books, 2011)

The Awakening to Light
(Leaf Press, 2010)

Cathedral (Ronsdale Press, 2010)

The Intelligence of Animals
(Backwaters Press, 2008)

Yellow Moon, Apple Moon
(Groundwood Books, 2008)

Stones Call Out
(Coteau Books, 2008)

The Crazy Man
(Groundwood Books, 2005)

Sky (Groundwood Books, 2004)

Poems for the Luminous World
(Frog Hollow Press, 2002)

likely
stories

PAMELA PORTER

RONSDALE

LIKELY STORIES
Copyright © 2019 Pamela Porter

RONSDALE PRESS
3350 West 21st Avenue
Vancouver, B.C., Canada V6S 1G7
www.ronsdalepress.com

Typesetting: Julie Cochrane, in New Baskerville 11 pt on 13.5
Cover Design: Julie Cochrane
Paper: 70 lb. Husky (FSC) — 100% post-consumer waste, totally chlorine-free and acid-free

Ronsdale Press wishes to thank the following for their support of its publishing program: the Canada Council for the Arts, the Government of Canada, the British Columbia Arts Council, and the Province of British Columbia through the Book Publishing Tax Credit Program.

Library and Archives Canada Cataloguing in Publication

Title: Likely stories: poems / Pamela Porter.
Names: Porter, Pamela, 1956– author.
Description: First edition.
Identifiers: Canadiana (print) 20190103256 | Canadiana (ebook) 20190103264 | ISBN 9781553805908 (softcover) | ISBN 9781553805915 (ebook) | ISBN 9781553805922 (pdf)
Classification: LCC PS8581.O7573 L58 2019 | DDC C811/.6—dc23

At Ronsdale Press we are committed to protecting the environment. To this end we are working with Canopy and printers to phase out our use of paper produced from ancient forests. This book is one step towards that goal.

Printed in Canada by Island Blue, Victoria, B.C.

for Rob, Drew, Cecilia and Chris

with much love

&

in memory of Patrick Lane

(1939–2019)

the heart lives,

even without its muscle

ACKNOWLEDGEMENTS

I want to extend my deep appreciation to everyone at Ronsdale Press: Veronica, Meagan, Julie, Chimie, and Ron for creating such carefully rendered and beautiful books. It is always a pleasure to work with you. I would also like to gratefully acknowledge the publications in which some of the poems in this book previously appeared:

"Notes: October" in *Arc Poetry Magazine.*

"Rupture" and "Aubade" in *Vallum.*

"Watching for snakes" in the League of Canadian Poets anthology, *Heartwood: Poems for the Love of Trees,* 2018.

"Emily and I" in the chapbook *The Precise Dimension of Light, Poems from Honeymoon Bay,* edited by Lorna Crozier, 2016.

"Portrait of the artist with Yu Xuanji (840–868)" in the chapbook *Choices, Poems from Honeymoon Bay,* edited by Patrick Lane, 2015.

"Robert Schumann" was featured on the CBC Music program, *In Concert,* on February 2, 2015, read by Paolo Pietropaolo.

"Photograph: Svetlana Stalin and her father" won the *Malahat Review*'s 50th Anniversary Poetry Prize, and appeared on the *Malahat Review* website, malahatreview.ca, 2013.

"In the clearing" in Coast Collective: In Conversation III, an exhibit of visual art inspired by poetry, April 2019.

*"The truth about stories is
that that's all we are."*
—THOMAS KING

— —

*"Sometimes we open our eyes in the
dark and nothing is the same."*
—PATRICK LANE

CONTENTS

– II –
I Dream a World

– III –
Delicate, Yet More Dangerous

The Wild Things

Sleep beneath a fruit tree not yet bearing fruit.
Let the wild things come to you.
Listen to their breathing, watch the feathers
rise and fall, the air leaving and returning.
Do the same as they. Then when you have
curled your body in this way for weeks, months,
for years, your eyes will become like theirs:
clear and able to see into the dark and to know
where the owl goes when she enters her
tunnel of dream.

− I −

Let Desire. Let Storm

Kanaree Caves, Salsette

Thomas Daniell, 1800, oil on canvas

Endure, endure, the Buddhas whisper, so slow
their stone tongues, so long they wait for speech.
They sleep much, and dream of light,
and like birds who remember a forest
they've never seen, would fly toward it
if they'd been carved wings. And like trees
that lie dormant in winter's endless rooms, they wait
for the hour which will receive them, hour upon hour,
and the one in which the painter will arrive
with his torch, and another, their flames two falcons
hunting down the shadows. As when you wait for a bell
which does not sound, and all you hear
is the absence of bell, the Buddhas listen with the keening
of those who are mute. But look —
how the painter's companion points toward their sky
where nebulae murmur to the new-blind stars —
and then the painter rises to leave, and the pointing man
who carries the torches, and the stars and nebulae
fold into the dark, and the Buddhas stand
watching the light go,
which is the same as letting go love, or grief, or hope,
because it is beating its wings in your hands,
because there is nothing else you can do.

Hunger

The men wander from table to table, one with a violin, one with a trumpet. Another holds a fat bass guitar which tilts toward the sky. Their women have sewn gold braid on their coats, their trousers. The tenor, tallest of them with thick black hair, might have sung in an opera if anyone had thought to travel this far to find him among scrub oak and trash and the sputtering candles in dark stone churches. He has, however, perfected the art of crying while singing. Against the clatter of forks and clamour for wine, the song begins about hobbled goats in a yard. Parched corn and a weary house. What will the children eat now? On the river, boats skim past without remorse. No matter the sadness, the trumpet turns it to joy. I came here exhausted, a hunger in my throat. But look, they are singing, there is light on the wall of the house. Sunlight falling in the doorway of the house.

Emily and I

Together in her drafty attic
we write our letters to the world.
Her lamp sputters, the light poor.

In the frame of her window the sun's last
spreads over Amherst's houses.

She let me in when I bragged I was nobody
and now sends me downstairs
to scrounge more paper —
envelopes, she insists — *envelopes.*

I creep down the creaky stairs.
Try to silence the swinging kitchen door.

Everyone's out but her pipe-smoking father
who won't spend a penny on paper.
He doesn't see my hand lift the wooden box
where he tosses the trash.

I sift out all the envelopes.
Take them up to Emily
and our fevered unfolding begins.

How she cringes when I make the tiniest tear.
This part takes time — the careful unhinging,
the smoothing.

She hands me a pen, an ink pot.
We go to work.

What I'll remember most
is her shadow on the wall — her hand,
and the pen large, swift,

and her hair — not pulled tight,
but down, free — almost, I would say,
wild.

Living with her

Grief walked in with her musty coat
and her grimy fingernails and will not leave.
She will not depart from any door.
She has made herself a bed on the floor
next to mine, beside the piles of books.
Some nights I wake to find her
reading the saddest poems.
She's the head honcho now.
She lays down the rules.
No glittering like the sun on water.
No singing. No marvelling at the sky.
No delicate teacups, dainty spoons,
no flowers in vases, no feeding the birds.
Until I am cleansed.
I ask when will I be cleansed.
But she is busy scraping the night of stars.

A litany for speaking

Because the wind bore down the house is dark
Because branches were flung from the trees
Because clouds broke free from the sky
Because sleep ran like a river fired with stars
Because the horse will not leave though the gate blew open
Because untamed birds have gone into hiding
Because the moon is dark and cold in its field
Because ceremonies must be offered
Because the soul is oracle for the heart
Because the soul speaks and the heart answers
Because nothing has been forgiven
Because forgiveness is waiting
Because you wait like a seed for the light to arrive
Because the ships are anchored in harbour
Because the storm on the water
Because he said it was his turn and he took it
Because the echo went out but did not come back
Because beginning to say no is not to offer so much a fist
                                   as a whisper of your name
Because it is your turn now
Because you waited on the light and it came as fire

Motif

Evening, the caretaker
with his rings of keys
comes to unlock the shadows,
releasing the many
darknesses.

Now, even the moon
will peer from behind
a curtain.

They say the soul
wears a shroud,
travels at night,
that the heart
works her own mathematics,
is most fond

of the broken:
the punctuated cry
of a loon,
a piece of music, violin
cut short,
the salt-polished
sea glass.

Portrait of the artist with Yu Xuanji (840–868)

Ink stone in one hand, brush in the other;
swallows wet-beaked from carrying mud.
I know — it's all about the poem.

There is something she needs to tell.
She has searched for the words all this time:
water fits itself to the vessel.
A pail, a pond, a world.

She liked plum and peach blossom together,
sang when no one could hear,
her flutes neglected in a corner of the room.
In this way we are one, Xuanji and I.

And that's not the half of it. I too believe
a little makeup hides imperfections, grief;
before you know it, suddenly you find
ten autumns have gone past.

Bamboo groves make worthy companions.
So do firs, a forest, rusty wire fence.
Out with my horses under the moon,
I don't need a lamp.
And you should see my books —
strewn everywhere, like yours.

How shall we care for the things of this world?
Feather by feather, stone by stone, blade by blade.
Each an illuminated manuscript,
a fallen bird, an open book the rain has found.

Open the cage. Let the crane fly free.

Lines in italics are taken from the poems of Yu Xuanji.

A woman's tale

My soul split into two one day. The confident half walked all around meeting people, and grew famous, while I stayed home and wrote poems. Then out of the blue, the confident one swaggered back. Asked what I'd been doing. Writing poems, I replied, and showed them. Turned out the other half of me had been writing poems, too. Hey, he exclaimed. You copied my poems. I did not, I said. How was I to know what you were doing, strutting back and forth out in the world. You stole my poems, said he. For a long time my soul stayed angry with itself. We were Hermione and Leontes. It was winter for years after that. I did not venture outdoors, and grew pale, ghostly, you could say, my skin translucent. And kept my poems secret from myself. To keep the peace.

Hermione and Leontes: characters in Shakespeare's *The Winter's Tale*.

The lost sister

When it was over,
the dam broken, the waters spilled out,
I shoved her aside, greedy for the life we both wanted.
My unborn twin
flew like a bird toward evening.
Now she calls to me, each cell of her
resplendent,
her hair the colour of sunrise.
She looks to be barely twenty.
Most days she is intolerably cheerful.
She says, see,
I told you to buy that horse. He's a good one.
You should listen to me more. You should listen.
Her slender finger, glittered as a comet,
wags at me.
Behind the rain, God knows where, the moon
is resurrecting itself.
A wren flits in the blackberry.
The silences she hears slip past my own ears.
She says, now listen up. I mean it. Get this down.

Interview

How far have you travelled?

It is said I was born with half a soul, beyond where the earth
is worn away, beyond dreams of the body and its roads
which lead under the sea.

Where is the other half?

The night begets sorrow, sorrow begets the branch
struck by wind, wind begets breath on the window.

Of what is the soul made?

Note the guard hairs of a wolf standing in snow.
Also, the startled, scraping leaves: a Pentecost of silence.

What part does the man play?

The rain, which remembers. The rain, ancient of days.
Inherited from the lynx who recovered it from the river stones
(even now grief seeks a place at the table).

And the burden of truth?

Borne by sparrows, juncos, chickadees,
the commonest of birds. In other circumstances
the sparrows would be mist, the juncos dawn, chickadees
a chatter of wind.

What passage did you use?

A door no longer a door, a door from which no one may enter
or leave, the space between two whales singing.

That would explain some things.

Yes, the silence which is a kind of music, a sound like wings
testing the air, which is to say, our memories, erased
as though they were dream.

Why is the bell important?

Something about the shape of the moon
when she has finished singing. And a clap with one hand
heard to the mountain and back.

What will sing beneath the earth now?

When the grasses are cut down and baled and stacked
into barns, when the bruised sky falls away to sleep,
fluttering delicate as moths. Don't ask what it means.
It is not for you to know.

Is that all?

As I wrote in the tongue of my ancestors, thread by thread,
with a hummingbird's breath and a pen which drew the narrow
rim of light above the hills. Look now — see
how the light there is changing colour.

Barbed-wire fence

Unreachable father, this
is despair:
to live always parallel to Earth,
a thin, grey line
binding the grasses in this field, one
small world: an acre of sky,
                    bursts of crocus, stone.

They imagine only what they have use for
and so have come to believe
you couldn't possibly exist,
missing the perfection of this garden
inside my embrace. Instrument
of the raw wind, rain, imagine
my sadness — the hard
weight of ice,
aware that I am not prized like the rose.

You write letters which no one reads,
draped like leaves, damp from the sending.
Animals leave their fur to me, the moon
her stony light.
Every day Death gleans this field,
pocketing her treasures. And you go on
doing whatever it is you do
which you call love.

Fragment of a letter found in an attic

in memoriam, George Lawrence Price,
15 December 1892–11 November 1918

The hour struck eleven. All warring ceased.
Sudden the silence that deafened us.
As per orders, we were not to fraternize.
Some nuns ran outside with flowers in their fists.
Who the hell knew where they got flowers.
In November, for Godsakes.
They pressed flowers into our hands,
flowers into the muzzles of our rifles.
Someone rang the church bell.
Drinks passed from hand to hand.
I looked all around — Hatfield was missing.
Where'd that bugger go?
Campbell found him finally in the church
playing the organ, giddy as a kid in a candy shop.
    Playing the goddamned organ.
But Price — two minutes to eleven for Chrissakes.
We buried him.
Rogers pulled out his bugle. All saluted the dirt.
Thus dismissed, we packed up what belongings we had,
and gradually understood we were going home.

Wing by wing

I know the spirits are rushing about when I can feel my hair scrape my forehead, though the air hangs windless. They gather their secrets into tight-lidded jars: recipes for roses, for tears; the date by which every hair on every head will be counted. The change they describe as a gale. It is coming they say, is nearly here, any moment now. It's building up. Atom by atom. Wing by wing. They draw sweeping motions through the air — the sign for patience. Have patience. You may have to wait years. The leaven in the bread may sleep longer than you ever dreamed possible. That is the care they take. A loss reveals a truth, many losses a life. But it is the prophecy they bury in the folds, in cobwebs, that the flutter of a monarch's wings will start the storm. Then we must let it, they whisper, let the air be disturbed. Let desire. Let storm. Let the stained-glass of their wings be opened.

Mrs. Einstein

You made me laugh when you started
threatening me with your recollections . . .
when someone is completely insignificant,
there is nothing else to say to this person
but to remain modest and silent. This
is what I advise you to do. —ALBERT EINSTEIN

Listen, Mileva — you can hear it: a sound
like rats scratching inside the walls
of your brain. One is the publisher
who erased you, left a single author
to the paper; another is Albert's mother
who says, at thirty you're an old hag,
you don't measure up. Mileva, you're a ship
rocking on the waves; your hands
grip the mooring rope day and night.
We have the letters, the ones
Albert wrote, tucked in the holds, some
for a century. How they boast of your brilliance.
Mileva, even faded ink cannot lie.
My tears will not prevent me telling you
some things have not changed.
It begins like this: you outscore all the boys
on the physics test. Including Albert.
On the oral portion the professor fails you.
No diploma for you, and that's that.
You can't overcome this, this
being a woman. No matter
the bare light bulb hanging from the ceiling,
the stove gone out, you and Albert
late into the night working; no matter
your part, your corrections to his math —
the sum belongs to him. Now

you're pregnant and still he won't marry you.
This ship is taking on water, Mileva.
Your first, a daughter, secreted away.
To this day no one can find her.
Then two sons you get to keep, one sent
to an asylum, where, penniless,
you lived with him. A bed on the asylum floor.
A schizophrenic and a woman unfit
for the world. Remember, Mileva — think
of the sirens who sang to the men
across the wine-dark seas, their hair
lifting in salt wind, the women
sages with hidden knowledge, their song
riding the drafts higher and higher,
the men chasing after.
When Mileva is no longer there, I can die in peace —
the letter scribed in Albert's hand.
If only for a little while, Mileva, for just an hour,
look down from where you are.
Here, I'll turn the pages. See
what they are saying about you now.

Packing grief

You pack your grief into a knapsack and set off on the trail, believing the picture before and behind you will do you some good. But in a short time the load grows heavy, not so much with the weight of it, but in the way it mocks you. So you set the knapsack on the stony ground, remove the grief to a boulder and walk on. The burden eases after that, and some sunlight begins to pour through windows framed by branches overhead. The grief, meanwhile, sits there in the forest. Anyone could pass by and take it home with them, but no one does. As you walk you begin to feel disloyal to the grief, that you and only you have betrayed it, left it slumped on a rock in an unsuspecting part of the forest. So you return to the place; you can spot it from a distance, and there it is, looking as miserable as ever. You stand around wondering what to do. Only your heart has the heart to pick it up as though it were an abandoned child; heart finds it in itself to forgive, and moreover, carry it home. And once home, you think the least you can do is to take responsibility and roll it into a quilt, frayed but clean. These days, you don't have to think about it so much. Only when there is some use for the quilt, like a picnic on the grass, for instance, when you lie watching the transient clouds float across that clear blue, as two eagles tumble over and over one another, locked together in the sky.

– II –

I Dream a World

Still-life

Andrew Wyeth paints Helga, 1975

The silence is an envelope
and the secret is folded inside it.
Even his wife does not know
that the housemaid from the nearby farm,
impossibly pale even in summer,
each morning slips quiet into the barn
where he keeps his canvases, his paints, and now
he is painting her, the sloped breasts,
the pubic mound. Her hair caught
in the light, a dusty window.
There is a discipline to the work.
It is difficult for her to hold so still
under the refinement of his eye, the attention
he gives to the curve of the ear.
A flock of geese cutting through the sky
distracts from the still life inside the barn.
How modestly the chin shadows her neck.
How the day holds its breath.
Cobwebs in the corners of the window
dare not move a filament. So brazen the sun
that blazes upon her nakedness.
The desire in his eye is spoken
by the brush. The mixture of tints
a striving for perfection, that is,
beauty. That he could be with her
in this sanctuary. That he must hide
the accumulation of her, the canvases.
Every morning she comes, undresses
in the furtive air, and the air's
fondness, and the light's secret hunger.

Moon, owl, stone

The maples test the air
by letting a few leaves go.
Each day I try to be grateful
for what is around me. The apple tree
ripening its fruit. The old horse
and the old man who keep on living.
I run on paths through the trees,
watching for loose rocks and roots.
And try to forgive all that needs forgiving.
I saw the moon travel in front of the sun.
I saw the moon's wild hair.
And an owl the colour of smoke
turned his head to look at me.
It was quiet then.
No one in nature made a sound.
There was darkness and then the light.
And with the light, awakening.
The story began with stars and the infinite
spaces of loneliness.
I'm talking about the old man.
Sometimes I have to forgive
all over again. I picked up a stone
the colour of the owl, stone
with the presence of the owl inside.
And took it home.
Set the table with bowl and spoon
and a cup for tea. And the stone.
All of us in unison spinning on the axis,
and the darkness that breathes inside everything.

Poem at the end of the year

The sky listens as horses pluck the blown grasses
with their teeth. High in the pines, ravens
sing the usual songs about the moon
            gone and come back changed,
ravens like dark gods so high up
they hardly notice us here on Earth.
I want the gods to know
            each day I try to be brave.
I look after horses, call them in from the field,
brush their coats until their skin
quivers with pleasure.
            I brush their manes and tails
and in this way try to nurture something of beauty
in the world.
            At night the gods send dreams
which they do not allow me to remember,
like the sea that pulls her spindrift down with her,
taking back each thing,
            wearing away the sand.
And wake at morning to songs of the shyest birds.

January

The moon lying in the water
moss climbing the trees
and the wild horse watching under the inexhaustible
bowl of night
and how we looked up
straight into the galaxy's spine

Ordinary singing

My unimportance does not keep
me from singing, nor the hawks
and grasses from listening.
The cats in the hayloft turn
onto their backs for me,
and the seasons, for the moment,
slow their turning. I do not need
to be a success in this life.
I need only to be awake to the world.
I need the heart to open.
The powers will keep holding
the Earth in their fists.
But the heart carries a sacrament
that is given and taken away,
a litany of breaking and mending.
In the dark hours poetry's bones
knit the broken things together
under shadows of the moon.
The owl, singing in poetry,
calls her mate in. Even if the gods
have never learned my name,
it does not keep me from singing;
I sing and it sounds to them like light,
like moonlight falling
among the branches of the heart.

Auction

The men are standing in dusty boots, spurs shaking as they
walk. They talk cattle, sheep, talk shearing, roping, as they
eye one horse, then another and another. They talk to the
handler. How many hands high. They say fifteen, fifteen-
two, fourteen-three. They say good reiner, a fine roper, say
the knees still good, talk hoof and frog and founder. Say,
this one'll go for a lady, look here now that's a right kind
eye; he's so gentle a child could ride 'em. And in the ring
the auctioneer starts his banter. Says sturdy, says strong
straight back, says young 'un, a keen learner. The men
with dusty boots look up into a sky without a lick of rain
and touch their hats, wipe their shirts. They're thinking
how their wives stared out the ranch house windows in
December with the dead eyes of a robin frozen to the
snow. Think she'd like that palomino as the banter trots
out: a good head, lot a years left in this 'un, never colicked.
The men watch from the bleachers, they stand at the fence
with one boot on the rail, scratch their heads with one
finger. Auctioneer says, you bought well but you might a
bought too soon. This one here, look a this appaloosa, just
might be the best one yet . . .

Telling the story

The leaves, the leaves all are flaming now, through the rains,
wet, gleaming, and after the rains the leaves still afire,
and the moon, having burned herself out, returns in the dark,

one thin slit of light she peers through, to follow our flaming,
lit by the strewn glitter of stars. An old man who is alive still,
told me the story, told it in the days before he turned stolid,

silent, but I remember how his voice was like unto the voice
of a god, but now I know it was only a man's voice, and he
but a man who would turn his back, would walk away

in the blink of an eye, and that is what he did. *Until
the lion tells the story, the hunter will remain the hero.*
It was what the man said. I reported the story too,

but my voice was that of a woman. Was doubted. But the lion
began bringing the lions together, meeting among the prides,
circled by the high grasses who whispered everything.

The lion spoke. Until they told their story, the hunter
would remain. And the birds listened with a careful ear,
and the flame trees, the lion standing on spread paws,

and the story went out. And the zebra spoke among the herd,
changing it to zebra, and the giraffe also, changing it just so,
and word spread, and the whale told the story over the seas.

And the rabbit, and the mouse — in each place the speech
again bravely spoken, and now among the trees, the leaves
are burning with it, even through the rains, as the moon

cups her bright ear to catch all parts of the story. The man
spoke as a prophet. But I, human, and woman, have not
a voice like the man, to be believed without question.

I have only this pen with which to tell you.

"Until the lion tells the story, the hunter will remain the hero" is a West
African proverb.

The way it breaks down

Two weeks after the baby is born my husband is called out to the coast for work. It is August and on the second day of his absence my three-year-old daughter surprises a rattlesnake which has found shade beneath the front porch. I pick up my daughter and rush into the house as the snake strikes at the boards under my feet. I call the neighbour from the next ranch and watch him barrel up the lane in his pickup, dust clouding the air behind him. Through the windshield I can see the outline of his Stetson as he nears the house. He has brought a high-powered hunting rifle which seems an inordinate amount of force for the task. The rifle blast wakes the baby who startles and cries. My daughter also wails in my arms. The man decides he will make a belt out of what is left of the snake and tosses it in the bed of his truck. In the house I set my daughter on the carpet in front of the TV and turn on *Mr. Rogers.* With the baby I go to the couch and unbutton my shirt to nurse. I am reading the testimonies of survivors from the bombings of Hiroshima and Nagasaki, a book from the local library stamped "Discard." My only chance to read is while I nurse the baby. I am near the end where the American flight crew speak. The pilot remembers a perfect morning, August 6, 1945. They'd named the plane *Enola Gay,* after Paul's mother. Five and one half hours flying over the sea. Seconds after they dropped the bomb the pilot cried out, *My God! What have we done?* I look up from the book. Mr. Rogers is talking to King Friday. They are trying to resolve a disagreement among the puppets. Our ranch is surrounded by 200 nuclear missiles stored in underground silos across central Montana, looked after by the Air Force, the missiles launch-ready, deployable at any moment. On the fourth day I awaken in the night to a blood-chilling scream, the windows open to let in the night air. I realize the scream must be from a cougar prowling the riverbank. Still, I go down the hall to check on my children, who, for the moment, sleep peacefully. August 9, 1945 was a mess from the start. Eight hours flying in monsoon wind, lightning, rain. The bomb broken loose, rolling around in the back of the plane. *Nearly everything went wrong that day. It almost didn't happen,* reported the co-pilot. On the sixth day I strap the children into their car seats and drive out of the valley toward town. Every missile is standing up out of its silo. Each one erect, pointing to the sky. There is no mention of missiles on the radio news. I check the paper. Nothing about missiles. For two days the missiles stand. By the third morning the missiles have been taken underground and sealed over by some high-ranking command. At the end of the book marked "Discard" is an explanation of the half-life of substances. The half-life of plutonium in the bomb dropped on Nagasaki is 24,300 years. The half-life of uranium 235 in the bomb dropped on Hiroshima is 700 million years. Half-life pertains to any chemical that is unstable in the way it breaks down. Every day on the television Mr. Rogers helps the puppets to solve certain problems, and he reminds the children that they are already acceptable as they are.

Robert Schumann

Watching a syncopation of sparrows
lined up like communicants
along the branch of the wild maple, I think of him
staring from the asylum window
toward the blackbirds on Endenich's church spire.

This morning the fir trees are still as cellos,
and I am remembering paw prints delicate
as an infant's hands, pressed into the wet silt
of the riverbank, and the way
wind flees sharp out of the mountains,
turning the river to a hard, white silence.

Music is everywhere. You can read the deer's antlers
like a score, a scapula washed up on stone, your own
heart's metronome the wrists echo, and the feet.

He took dictation from hooves on cobblestone,
the goat man's *arpeggio,* the *glissando* of rain
that rose past the locked door of his second floor room.
Angels visited him there, then demons.

I know this: in the low place outside the periphery of fence
sleeps a cougar.
My horses stand rigid, alert when he passes unseen.
Should he be sighted, he'll be shot, though his green eyes
hold both Perseus and Cygnus in a moonless light.

Turning with the Earth

Between past and future, spring and winter,
I live my life. Between having, and the purity
of not having. I cannot keep straight all the gods
and goddesses who hiked through Hades
and back, and who strung a lyre with strands
of the sun. But I know what Salome asked for
and received; I know where Thomas went after
he was called out for doubting. I don't doubt
what the man thought of my poems.
I just wish he would tell the rest of the world.
Almost past winter now, the trees are still
dreaming their lost children, and the Earth
has turned so far, she will never be herself again,
though the heart still loves and breaks,
breaks yet still loves. What can we expect
of the old men who turn frail and refuse
to become our fathers, to guide us out
from beneath the shadows? Today
in the afternoon the owls gathered
and sang in the pines, enough to be a choir.
All the different pitches.
If there was no message, there was music,
a kind of sacrament I could live on a long time,
could live on beauty and music alone.

Easter Sunday

Andrew Wyeth, water colour, 1975

She stands on the farmhouse porch
in her green cape coat, looking out
on a hill snow-covered
but for a strip of bare ground
formed not by sun, but by wind.
Wind beats a tree's branches
against the house. The sky, white.
The long slope of the hill, white.
In her mind are crocus,
then lilacs, and after, roses.
But the heart believes in the possibility
that what mind calls memory
is only dream, and that the day
may have come when the season
will no longer change. Time stops;
for a moment, or for years,
we live in eternity. And the woman,
pale in her loden coat, who cannot
see into distance. And the soiled
white-painted porch. And the memory
faint enough to seem unreachable.
Crocus, then lilacs. And after, roses.

Something completely understood, but unspeakable

I had driven nearly to the border.
The road signs had switched languages.
Heat, a pressing down, registered inside me.
It said my life would be altered.
It said I would be purified.
On the road, dust rose like the spirit flying into heaven.
Falling up to the blinding light.
Something I carried left me then.
Some long skin rubbed off in the underbrush.
A large snake ribboned across the sand, then vanished,
but its pattern remained like an ancient script
whose meaning lay, over centuries, undeciphered.

Girl walking backward

In the days that follow, she does not speak,
refusal her first and last word.
No matter their demands, their shouting at her,
she remains steadfast.
The sea fills her mouth.
A wilderness builds its nest inside her.
She walks backward into silence.
She had not known parts of her could be lost.
Could be taken.
Hidden within the *no* is a gate broken open.
Folded inside the *I am* is the erasure.
There are horrors that are visited upon young girls.
Some acts are not measurable.
Her body not ready for blood, yet there is blood
in a place only she knows. In a place it should not be.
The gods who live in the house decide
nothing is wrong with her.
They say she needs to straighten up.
Already a piece of her has flown.
She watches its wings, frail, vanish over the roof tops.
She knows it is never coming back.

A likely story

As a child I fell ill with pneumonia year after year, strangely, in the heat of summer. I had not yet beheld an entire field of yellow, but I dreamt it then. The sky, hard, blue, nevertheless was patient with me, as in my fevered sleep others approached my bed whom decades later I would meet — one whose voice made me think of leaves scraped by wind; one whose eyes were the black ponds by which the moon each night regarded herself; and one whose head was obscured by swirling snow which I recognized only from drawings in my storybooks. When, after years I came upon each in human form, I remained too astonished to speak. It was clear each had no memory of me. Granted, I had changed much since childhood. Once, I approached the subject of our earlier meeting with the one who spoke in a voice like leaves, an exchange which did not end well. Still, a certain grace has accompanied me. Even now I dream a world in which the stars call to each other, a sound like a band of foxes answered by a loon, followed with a silence which I have known only when looking on a field entire of yellow, beside another field, an expanse, blue; which, if one were not aware, might mistake the field of minute, sky-coloured blossoms for a vast inland sea.

Dignity

The constellations revealed themselves
in the space surrounded by immense firs.
But she was bewildered by so many stars
and their ancient stories,
and whether she could unearth
the myriad secrets. Finally she understood
it was not her fault. Truth was,
she was not believed.
Mornings she watched the goldfinch, fledged,
feathers disarrayed, and remembered
how long it took her to learn
what other kids got at home, like how not
to look like you just rolled out of bed.
Left alone in the stillness, she saw
her reflection: a weed rustling
where flowers grew, and that hard blue overhead.
Surprisingly, her heart did not wither.
She carried the weight, her hunger
but also light, as fallen onto the adobe wall,
and the precise shadow of winter trees.

3:56 a.m.

The moon
has pulled her curtain aside
and like a Holy Ghost
unfurled a stream of light across
the yard
I think of my horses
down by the barn
the cats curled in the hay
if they are as overcome
by contentment
as I

Where the road ends

keep walking toward the rusted barbed-wire gate. Lift
the wire latch stapled to the post, then lay the gate down
against a snarl of blackberry. Walk the potholed path
wide enough for a hay truck to stumble through, past
the only house at the end of the road, past the creek
running high in winter, in flood, the skeleton trees
and a rusted pipe through which the creek passes beneath you,
then breaks free beyond the nurse log and the stump wide
as a farmhouse table where saplings, cedar, sprout, and now
there's a proper gate of pipe and hinges and a chain latch,
and an overcast sky that will bury the stars in the next
short hour, and here is the old Morgan pony to greet you.
The other horses prick their ears; the younger, a bay, whinnies.
You head for the barn your kids painted one summer
in primary colours, the roof invaded with moss, wedged
in shadow, and you pry open the door and go in and prop open
the plywood window. The horses stamp their hooves
as you section flakes of hay off a bale and feed them
through the window, while you're thinking of what
went on last night inside the house, what your son
said to his father, how each flared sudden, like a match,
how each left the table one by one, when out of the dusk
an owl calls like forgiveness, and there's a quiet, broken
only by horses nuzzling hay, and the owl again, and silence.
Then, in another part of the falling dark, the reply.

– III –

Delicate, Yet More Dangerous

Instructions for the apotheosis

You are the lost daughter, taken from sleep, smuggled
from one country into another by a man
who speaks deeply, rarely.
Who, upon reaching the border, will claim you are his wife.

Together you traverse dangerous terrain, the winds
northern, sharp, your poems carried in secret,
furious with dream, sewn into the lining of your coat.
You have taken all precautions:
your passport's photo and your own face altered,
as if to say, *she is no poet.*

Often you go hungry, and once or twice are taken in
by strangers bearing false names.
You believe the man will abandon you once
he discovers there is no one willing
to pay your ransom.

While crossing a forest, the night's heartbeat,
moonless, the authorities ambush you
with flashlights, batter you with questions
in a dialect you do not understand.
You look them in the eye, feign innocence.

Miraculously, they let you go.
A foreigner in the new country,
nevertheless you pass as one of them, but fear
your accent will betray you.

Years pass, and one day a master, proficient in his art,
takes you into his charge, instructs you
in the subtler aspects, your work
grown finer, delicate, yet more dangerous

until he accuses you of forgery, a concocted charge,
and you must flee, keep silent even among
your small network of comrades
who, unsuspecting, fail to protect you.

Show them your wrists.
To say you were not harmed would be a lie.
You hold private ceremonies of desolation,
the bells that could not, would not ring for you.

Over time you make your home in a clearing, the wild
your neighbours, solitude your companion.
As for your art, harboured all the far distances,
concealed like children beneath your cloak —
well, paper is a fragile thing. Ink fades.

No matter. The fire-burned end, a sharp stick will do.
Begin with *breath*.
Continue: *touch*.
Hold the stick once more to the fire.
You won't be silenced.
Never again will you be silenced.

Becoming a poet

It's what you've come to.
Spindrift, moon dust, breath. So that
they who ply their carts in the grocery aisle
nearly pass right through you, though you're
hauling the world's detritus behind you:
wreckage from bad weather and greed, shattered
faces crying out for mercy. This
is what becomes you, what you've become,
most at home among the spectacles of darkness
and its opposite, though friends who've lost
the way to your house, or never think to come,
still might find you there, more soul
than substance, cirrus than cumulus.
Your life's calling: to hover between the trash heaps
of this world and another, better, that greeting
flung into space still waiting on an answer.
Here, even strangers take to staring
at your veins running clear as a map beneath your skin,
and could find your heart, if you let them,
floating in its cage like the swim bladder of a fish
that keeps you upright and standing just so on Earth,
a moon for the muses to carry down the mountain,
resembling at first a skull, or pottery, ancient,
unearthed. Or that having become your art,
the vessel, the flesh broken open,
some invisible grasp that holds you to this gravity
could turn you in at any moment — double-crosser,
a turncoat — sell you out. And some days, you'd go,
relieved, let the tide take you, but for the music
you hear in the hills at dawn, a howling like sirens singing,
the warp and weft of it, muzzles raised to night's fading.
And how the pines, sudden, set themselves on fire.
Get up. Drink. This is what you're here for.

The trail up to Hidden Lake

Tamaracks stood
as though in flame
and the moon a blossom
rose dark as parchment
as wet stone
and we saw how much had been given us

Families don't exist here

Families don't exist here.
—U.S. BORDER AGENT, TORNILLO, TEXAS

It is a child prison camp.
—SEN. JEFF MERKLEY, VISITING TORNILLO, TEXAS

*You are no longer strangers and aliens, but citizens
and members of the household of God.*
—PAUL OF TARSUS

It is the room you make inside yourself,
where the roof, canvas or otherwise, disappears,
because it's your room and you
                        are eight years old
and can make it vanish at your will.
Instead of a roof, canvas or otherwise,
in place of the air-conditioned cold, glint
                    the migrant stars
who see everything, and the moon
who watched you each night getting here,
                    and clouds
dragging their long white silences.
Where God, a child today,
plays dead behind the razor-wire fence.
                       God, who arrived
disguised as hunger, as thirst.
                Each day tells its tale to another,
a story in which everyone you love
has disappeared as though in mist.
                There is no use for memory here,
that repository against loss;
          language grows wings, slips
             through the chain link of your cage.

Only your heart stays behind,
                    curled in its nest of bone.
And God counts on her many fingers
all the ways the world
                    has closed its fists to you,
a door no child may enter or leave from.
Years from now you'll wake again
from the dream
                    you cannot put behind you —
the tyrant sun, slice of shadow, risen dust.
And a sound of wings beating the air.

Witness to the spill

after Ruth Stone

Eye of sky
droop dark,
darkly net
slip light.
Wing wet
feather furl
beak black
nit nit nit.
Flee! Flee!
Come nought!
Feather fur
fin frond
key-a-key,
too-wheeeeee.

Translation:

Night fell and caught us in his net. Our wings wet,
beaks black, we could not fly. And to them who circled
over us, we cried, Save yourselves! Warn feather, fur;
warn fin, frond: the prophecy of old, the stories of our
ancestors, the prophecy has been fulfilled.

Migration

Tijuana, Mexico, November 2018

As I wrote in my first language, in the beginning
we kneeled, dipped water from the shallow rivers
into our hands. Now there is no water.
We are but crumbs in the world's pocket,
following a map creased, stained and torn,
earth and sky reflected in our bones.

Week by week walking over stones and shards of glass,
our sentences translate from sorrow to despair.
The children's feet are bare. Even the moon
grows thin and has stopped eating. Each night
the bruised sky falls away to sleep, and we wake again,
the pierced morning, the crucified world.

Everything else you have to imagine for yourself.
Arrived at the border, thousands of us, we wait.
And then the soldiers release the gas.
This I have learned at great cost: how grace
is withheld for no reason you can fathom.
In my hand is the pen that scrapes our conclusion.

I am your sister, your daughter; I am history's recorder.

Getting through the war

Nicaragua, 1988

The only way to the village is by a road washed out
from the rainy season, but you go anyway,
standing in the bed of a truck, holding on
to the wooden slats. Dust covers you and the heat
stings your skin. You could sit on the sacks of beans
stacked behind the cab, but you are pregnant,
and to sit is uncomfortable, so you stand with the others
the whole two hours. When you arrive in the village
a man helps you down, and the women point
their chins at you and say, *embarazada.*
Small girls cover their mouths and stare.
The work is to stack bricks that have dried in the sun,
the people starting over after the Contras came
and burned everything. It takes strength, after a fire,
to get up, make tortillas, feed the kids, all
the everyday things. In thirty years you'll ask yourself
if what you found there is still true.
You grow dizzy hauling bricks in the heat. The women
lead you down to the river where they show you
how to scrub clothes on large white stones. The river
is clear and cool, your skirt billows in the water,
and the women smile, pointing out your hair.
Brillo del sol, they say. Colour of sunset. Like flame.

Embarazada: Spanish, to be pregnant.

Pale wanderer

Dead, the pine, burnt out in the summer fires,
and so close to the house; and the field
of dry grasses near and perishable, but spared
who knows how or why, and I thought, hoped
even, that a raccoon might claim the charred
trunk for her brood, faces poking out, curious,
but no raccoons came. Instead, dusk fell early,
October, the garden or what was left of it, failing,
the pine's branches blacker against the black night.
And then the moon with his wild smell, furtive
animal, pulled himself over the rim of the world
with no great struggle; effortless it seemed, this rising,
a fluid thing. I waited for him there at the edge
of the wood, one part of him singed, too,
the fires having eaten the mountain, the hills,
and it was then I heard him snuffle in the branches,
was then I held out my palms, open. Fearsome
his visage. Nevertheless, I loved his bright face.
The silence growled soft when he came near,
settled in the pine for the while that he did.
His snout wet when he sniffed my hands.
But I could not hold him, nor tame him.
A night bird screeched afar off, the mist
formed and rose. Startled, he slipped away. I confess
I wanted him for myself, craved his obeisance,
this being with bruised face that would not heal,
who knew nothing of love, neither old nor young,
neither furred nor winged.

Entreaty

poem for two voices

Einaudi's horses bolt across the piano,
      his music a cloud of dust.
Soon our loved ones will vanish into songbirds,
      without my sadness,
While prairie barns fall down in their fields
      of wheat, and the old houses,
and even if my days were emptied of love and flutes,
      emptied of silence,
while God pulls away the sky to night's
      shattered glass, and the famished moon
that is sweeter than grief, my parched tongue, the day
      crushed like bone,
swells and blossoms, and all who have lost
      their way, stretch their necks,
and wonder, if the dead, no longer prisoner,
      still chew the bitter root,
climb the cliffs for a better view, filaments
      of stars in their eyes.
asking, is there consolation for life's brevity?
And taking their faces in my hands, I implore,
      write to me where you are.

Predator

Something's spooked them.
   Something that crept past in the underbrush,
      or brasher, tracked straight across the meadow.

Even the grandfather of the herd, the sorrel, has flung up
   the winter-wet sod, cut hoof-shaped moons into the soil.
      The bays are bumping into each other, backing away;

no noise from their throats, no snorting out their nostrils.
   Sound and fear must not betray them.
      Some scent set off the limbic brain, and now

they are the herd returned to the steppes,
   odour of tiger, toothed, or cougar — the same
      spine, shoulders urging the wide paws forward,

and the eyes — it is enough.
   They hardly settle to eat when I put the hay out.
      Their skin still rippling. Ears forward, taut.

They look up, stare hard into the pines.

As above, so below

February and snow still clinging to the grasses, snow lining the branches overhead as night rides the shoulders of my barn coat smeared with dirt, bits of hay hidden in the pockets and turned-up cuffs. Clanking the gate's chain latch, I watch the Big Dipper float over the tips of the pines like a great hay trough where the sky horses gather to feed. Clouds stretch past like dust in a summer drought. If someone dared to ask what is the sound of the sky horses running loose in night's prairie, what answer could I give? Only snow answers to the moon tonight. Only they sing to each other the same bright song.

The bell

When the old horse loses his sight,
I bell the younger horse so the blind one
does not cry out in fear.
The field goes on being the field. The fences
go on holding them as the sky listens
in the keep of its stillness.
The horse believes in the bell that calls him
to grass he feels with his hooves,
the pasture ancient as a temple.
There is an infinity to them; there is an ocean.
Their nostrils fill with the scent of pine
that stand wild and blind at the edge
of the wood, where owls find each other,
singing at the close of day, dreaming
their music even before it leaves them,
a bell that pierces the darkness, a star
alighted on a branch of its constellation.
All night the horses sleep
neck over curve of the other's back,
breathing the other's breath, their heads
leaning against the dark. All night
I listen for the glittering sound of bell
as the young horse shifts his weight in sleep.

Perspective

Should you find yourself on Mars, craning your neck toward the butterscotch sky, note that at the end of day as the fierce blue sunset fades, that evening star you see, that *pale blue dot,* is Earth. Look past the two cat-eyed moons above you — there it is, rising. If you have a telescope handy you can also find Earth's moon. What mote of loneliness it must seem — this Earth with its lumbering moon circling like a distant lover, for eons unrequited. What you can't see from the dusty soil you're standing on is the way the stars fall there at certain times, hidden under clouds — stars in great clusters, grown cold, and gravity pulling them down and down toward the stiff and frozen soil. Uninhabitable, you might say. And who are you to be here, at this distance, this moment of breath? And what will you tell the others? That birdsong, if there had been a song, would be swallowed up before the song was done? That you heard the silence, felt the great shiver at the heart of the universe? And now you are certain, as you wait inside your own pulse, that all is born of the one heartbeat, the pinpoint — that's you. But then, anything you can point to is the centre of the universe. So, how did you get here, and how will you make it back to that evening star?

Shepherds

We offer here our testimony.
Scribes, yes, combed the countryside for witnesses,
        and paralyzed by certainty, dismissed our deposition.
This is what we saw.

The madness of weather, sand's fury, and after,
            the stultifying air; we cleaved
to low places, any watercourse, however meagre;
shelled out bribes, when cornered,
            to armoured men on armoured horses.
The sun's laborious voyage across the sea above, nomad
                sheep in migratory drift.
Time on our hands, time beneath our feet,
            time crevassed over time into our skin.
And we watched. Witnessed the event. Forewarned
            when a crazed and sordid thing
of the prophet lot — cadaverous, crawling with lice —
staggered into camp, made a nonsense of speech,
and like sand in the eyes, maddened us; we left him
    snoring near a fire, a grimy scrap of bread, olives,
                the wail of wind.

But recognized the couple, yet far down the valley, took note
of the burdened animal, cloven explosions of sand
            forced from the cloven hooves.
Dusk advanced. The man's insistent feet, the town epidemic
with stale smells of wine and urine and bitterness.
We saw them turned away, turning toward the barn.
                Across the way,
the flophouse ran a steady business.

Truth is, we were first to bear him gifts —
things we considered a boy would desire:
                three stones of intriguing stripes and colours;
a coin picked out of the dust;
a fistful of dried strung gut, and two wooden spools
which would serve for wheels;
                and dingy fleece caught in tangled brush,
spun between thumb and forefinger in the tedious watch,
string rolled into string to make a ball — those things
his mother, no doubt, would pull from his pockets.
                It was what we thought he wanted,
what we had, and laid before him on the straw.

We testify to this: that we met him
                before royalty arrived at last
with their erroneous sextants. They'd crossed, far
off-course, and finding themselves here by chance,
unloaded the weighty gifts along with their self-importance.

Truth is, we shouldn't have needed him at all, not
                if we had trusted our own sight.
Even he couldn't save us from ourselves,
                though the inchoate cried out for it, in the towns
and cities, in the villages, that is,
                before they set on him at the end.
But there were years they strung after him as he walked,
                pointing out this thing and that —
                                mind you, simply noticing.
Sparrows. Sheep. Lilies in the field — extravagant, serene.

He only showed them what was here all along.

See you

My elderly friend calls, asks me to a movie, says her sister told
her to go; it's about finding love late in life, and my friend, in
her seventies, wants to find it, so I go with her, thinking this
won't have much to do with me, but the title, *I'll See You in My
Dreams*, should have been a warning, that the movie is really
about grief, and release, because first off, Blythe Danner has to
put her dog down, and already I'm in tears because I've done
this too many times to count, but my friend is hoping that
Blythe will actually find love at her age, and she does — with a
kind, silver-haired man with a silver moustache, and when
they're in bed together I see that my friend is grinning and
wiping her face, because it's possible now, it could happen to
her, too, but even the lovers aren't spared, because the movie is
really about death, sudden and inexplicable — about outliving
nearly everyone you've ever loved, and there's a young man,
too, who can't be more than thirty, who cleans her swimming
pool, who writes poetry — he really loves her, but hasn't got a
chance; he's more like a son, but not her son, so he loses on
both counts, and by the end, we see Blythe at the pound looking
in the cages at all the dogs, we see her driving home with a
round-eyed mutt in the front seat — the dog, we're told, is
twelve years old, and we know where this is headed, but it's
those moments of joy, of pure love that we'll give anything for;
it's why we open ourselves again and again, why we let them in.
We've all done it. I know I have.

– IV –

A Long Road
into Dawn

Photograph: Svetlana Stalin and her father

She is seven and smiling, caught
in the crook of her father's arm.
His hand cups her chin,
his sleeve envelops her,
and she must believe, as small girls do,
that he is close to God,
the sun bright as a watch
              he keeps on a chain.

Behind them waits a regiment of trees,
and behind the trees a wide field, geese,
a lake white with swans,
and beyond in the far city,
verdigris domes
where, inside, candles flame,
because the day has turned to winter
and there is a sound of boots in the streets;
because the trains are full
and lurch across the snow
into the open mouth at the edge of the world.

It is what small girls learn, curled
toward sleep in their beds:
a man brushes past his daughter
and without kiss or touch, goes out
into darkness, a door
shut quiet behind him.

If I could light a lantern
and show her a photograph of her future,
the dead refusing silence,
trains rusting under snow and the blighted
                              circle of the moon,
and she carrying his name like iron,
all the questions would remain the same:
who is God? And what is love to do then?

The present moment

Snow all day, and now dusk, and the horses are rearing and bucking and galloping; even the old one canters a clean circle, head tucked, hooves spraying snow. I open my hand and thrust it in air, meaning, in horse language, go away, give me room, and they keep a distance while light lifts from the tips of the firs, dissolves into the night. And the dog, racing past the fence line, sends a raccoon up a tree and she's barking her instinctive high-pitched yelp. Weather has set them off. And now with hay set out, and buckets of feed, I call each horse by name, and they come, and quiet settles in. From the beginning I knew how to feel this place: scent of cedar, the curve in a branch that turns to claw, to owl, how night roams lonesome as the two bucks just come into the clearing, and now hoof prints — moon-shaped and cloven, paw prints and boot prints lie spread like constellations in the snow. And now the sky brings forth its own.

In the clearing

All morning the raven pair
inked the sky with their spread wings.
And spoke to each other with a sound
like water dripping into the trough.

And bent the cedars with their weight,
and eyed me in the way wild things do.

All morning the past bulged my pockets.
And forgiveness has come at last
to the one who has forgiven.

It is happening now: the world
broken into its parts: light and dark,
the possessed and dispossessed.

And the raven pair riding the sky,
talking their watery talk.
And the sky, having neither wings nor feet,
settles weightless on the earth.

Not yet spring; no wind in the trees.

Watching for snakes

Robert E. Lee Junior High, Monroe, Louisiana

The path to school lies
through forest, through underbrush
and blackberry.

A narrow path,
with scarcely room enough for a child
in your canvas shoes.

You remind yourself, *keep an eye out.*
Watch for snakes. A broken
music turns in your head. A rag
of wind braids your hair.

Vines hanging from the oaks
are sturdy enough to swing on.
You know because you've done it.
But you're late again, and try to hurry.

This is *before.*
After will be for all time.
For eternity.

You step into the clearing
just as the bell sounds.
This is still *before,*
but time and your feet do not stop.

And now. *Now.*
You see it.

In the night perhaps,
or early, early this morning
in the schoolyard

some of the boys have tied
a rope into a noose,
hung the noose in a tree.

A crowd has gathered.
The principal has not come
to take it down.

They did it, the boys,
to threaten the children
arriving on busses,

whom the President
spoke of on television
when he ordered
that the races must mix.
That there be no separation.

Hunched at your desk
in the humid classroom,
for all you know
the noose is still there.
Nuzzled by the wind.

All day, in your mind
the noose is hanging from the tree.

Now it is *after*.

When the school bell
dismisses you for the day
you walk outside
to see that the rope is gone.

But in *after,*
the rope will remain,
for all time, in the tree.

After, as in *forever after,* as in
unchanged and unchanging, Amen,

and it is as though you
are no longer a child,
but one of the witnesses
of whom it was written in the gospel:

But she was deeply troubled by this
and hastened away,
and told no one what she had seen.

Notes: October

Hay poor this year.
Took 2nd bag of weeds to Tom.
Told him weeds thick in 15 bales
so far.

    Underline *so far.*

Connemara arrived, black mane
and tail. Shoes on both front feet,
packs up wi. rocks & mud.
Have to clean out wi. hoof pick.
Will ask farrier to pull shoes.

    Check mark beside *farrier.*

Put Connemara in paddock wi. Shetland.
Dominance wars ensued.
Must separate by gate when eating,
come back after dark to open gate.
Don't want to do this forever.

    Circle *forever.*

Picked up manure in heavy rain.
Pine needles floating in water trough.
Wheelbarrow piled wi. wet manure & mud.
Felt dazed by rain, isolated, alone.
Found shard of blue china in mud.

    Draw box around *blue.*

The old sorrel keeps clear
of the Connemara, grazes
opposite corner of pasture.
Only 2 months ago dragonflies,
dust, Queen Anne's lace.

Add *memory*, add *momentary*.

Two maple trees gone bright red.
Was it sudden or did I fail to look?

Circle *look*.

Connemara wins dominance war.
No need to separate now.
Peace breaking out.

Exclamation mark after *peace*.

Scrubbed water trough after storm.
Raised pump handle wi. both hands.
Water rushed sunlit, cold.
Felt hopeful again.

Circle all of it.

Took Connemara on trails first time.
Wind swirling after storm, branches
cracking. Connemara unalarmed.

Two check marks after *unalarmed*.

Only thing growing now: darkness.
Checked temperature. Took flashlight,
blanketed 3 horses. Put out more hay.
Stars out, slivered moon.

Circle *moon*.

A kind of victory

He is back, he has returned, he is
at my front door with yellow
squash in his hands. A gift.
A consolation prize for the years,
the abnegation. But here he is
in the flesh, hair white, eyes dim;
time has put him to the test, I think.
And I let him in, I turn
unforgiveness into forgiveness.
He wants to turn injustice
into justice and I say to myself
Hallelujah, open all the doors
and windows, let sister justice in,
let her rap her gavel and declare
a new day. This is him, I'm thinking,
in his skin, sipping tea, admiring
the grand piano. Do I remind him
how I invited him to come
hear this piano, and he refused?
And now he's slumped a little, his
fingers laced over his stomach,
a bit awkward, when he brightens
and asks me to play. Do I remind him?
But I sit down at the keys
and begin. *Für Elise.*
All of it. The whole mysterious,
shadowy realm of it, as though
the world were covered in ice
and evening has fallen early
and one must accept the darkness,
inevitable, because it will be
a long road into dawn.
A long road.

Judgement

She believed the man who said
her poems were copies.
It was as though the two of them
were characters in a play, dressed
in the costume of an earlier time.
And he onstage, delivering his soliloquy
while holding a sheaf of her poems.
For a while she believed him.
Until scene III. And still
no lines had been written for her.
She had no tactic for impromptu.
Outside the theatre the moon rose
behind the pines, casting long shadows
which were like the spread wings
of predator birds.
By the second act it was clear
the play was a tragedy.
She knew then there are finalities
other than death. After a time
she gathered up her poems
and distributed them among the needy.
The quiet then, and the clarity,
like a slant of light,
as the poems lay claim to their truth.

Renouncement

At dusk in the ruined light the horses buried in the field rise and graze with the others. The ghost horses are indistinguishable from moonlight, or the sound of air beaten down by owls' wings, or shells washed up on the sea. She watches from a distance and they know she is there, the one who fed them, and when she had no choice, buried them. Though it is only August, already leaves have gone yellow. Already the light closing down. Leaves like souls who have given up and let wind take them. In the poor light the ghost horses flare their nostrils at the smell of earth, and the first stars swish their pale white tails.

Between

In my mind I go back
to that place near the border.
Scrub mesquite. Heat in November.
A few people drove up the dirt road.
Parked at the cafe. But where
they came from I did not know.
And the light fell onto everything
except the porch where shade
took on precise angles,
and also beneath the pickup trucks.
We ate quietly, as though
it were a wayside stop between
this country and the next one.
Those who arrived were getting
used to the light, so that we
could bear more light, and the emptiness
that was coming into us.

A theory

It was the rattlesnake took down
the eagle in flight —
the eagle having
dived down the steep
air toward the field,
its eye on
the snake and the snake
snared in the great
talons. Yet the claw,
dug in too far from
the head and the head
flung back, buried
its venom in
the leg and both
tumbled from
the sky, and tangled,
lay dead in the
dust road, the feathers
lifting, and the snake
still, and still
holding on.

She wasn't perfect, but she was perfectly Knowlene

On Tuesday Knowlene Edwards drove her truck into town and came back dead. It wasn't the first time, either. But this time she recognized it right away when she found herself floating in the sky, watching her body steer the long, dry road, elbow out the window, the windshield picking up bugs. And her first thought was, *Damn*. She couldn't see God up there, but it didn't matter. That was it: nothing mattered. *It's the same*, she thought, *rain or sun or moon or black of night*. And the fields in wheat, green just starting to turn, looked like a famous painting she saw once on TV. Also with the river, and Stanley's bulls out grazing the pasture. And from on high, on neighbouring farms, she watched Jack working to jump that poor excuse for a tractor, Ray walking down to the PO, and Marvelle inside, sorting mail into all those little boxes. How they seemed like birds to her, opening and closing their wings, poking around in their disguises, yet innocent as grass. What puzzled her most was how she could be dead and looking all around while part of her still kept the truck on the road. And then quicker than death itself, she was back in the truck, behind the wheel, turning into the lane, and her dog chasing the truck home. She lay awake nights after that, trying not to forget, playing it over and over in her mind.

Raylene gets fed up

Mama yanks me hard by my hair and says, *Just wait till your father finds out, young lady*, after catching me and Toby Sykes holding hands behind the fellowship hall. We ain't even to the car and Mama gets her scowl on and says, *You tryin' to get yourself pregnant?* Well, nobody, not no one ever said you could get pregnant just holding hands. Soon as we come home Mama sends me to my room and I wait a long, long time till her and Daddy decide what to do with me. Then Daddy come in and folds his hands thoughtfully in front of him and says, *Raylene, I want you to pray about this. You need to ask the Lord to forgive you for the sin which you have committed.* Then Mama come in, picks up my Bible that's sitting on my dresser, slams it down on the bed in front of me and says, *When was the last time you opened your Bible? I advise you to read it, little Miss. Read what the Bible says about what happens to girls who hold hands with young men.* Well, for number one, I read my Bible every day. I colour in with pencil crayons the parts I like best: *You are the light of the world. Let justice roll down like water, and righteousness like an ever-flowing stream.* And for number two, Toby Sykes is my age. Thirteen. With acne. I wouldn't exactly call him *a man*. Then of course, my sister Darla's got to stick her head in the door and whisper, *I heard what you did, stooooo-pid!* So I stayed up half the night reading all Matthew, Mark, Luke, John, the Acts of the Apostles and Paul's letter to the Romans. I swear there's nothing in there about holding hands with thirteen-year-old boys. Just Paul, who was probably a grumpy old man anyhow saying wives should submit to their husbands. Darla says that means they get to do anything they want to us and we have to let 'em. Well I never seen Darla hold hands with no boy. She's tight with her little group of girls. Darla always seems like more boy than girl anyhow. Just keep your ears open when Mama tries to get Darla in a skirt. You'd be convinced she was a wildcat in distress. But Mama usually gives in and lets her wear pants even though the church says girls must wear dresses. See, we don't go to regular school. We go to the school our church set up and the Law is always coming by to see what they're teaching us. You can bet your britches they don't tell us in school where babies come from. I asked Faith Jennings once and she just pointed between her legs. I do know about starting your period 'cause I already got mine and Darla got hers before that. Nobody told me Darla got her period but I could tell just by what ended up in the bathroom trash. When I got mine, I showed Mama my underwear, and was she ever mad. She made Daddy drive her all over town to get the right equipment. And then when they come home Mama didn't explain nothing. I had to read the instructions on the box to figure out what to do. In school they showed us a film about getting your period 'cause the Law says they have to. Mama believes Darla is the righteous daughter who's gonna grow up and be the kind a woman who submits to her husband, and I'm headed for she-don't-know-what. Daddy says it's because of people like me that modern folk don't live as long as people in the Bible. *Sin*, Daddy says, *pure and simple.* Me, I look out my bedroom window at the clouds passing and the trees, and folks driving past and I tell myself someday I'm gonna go out and see what the rest of the world is like. I'm gonna start walking. And if I like what I see, I ain't never, ever coming back.

They called him Wing

If you'd been walking by our farm that day, or been
a stranger driving down the road, I'd have looked
for all the world like a girl running from a barn,
my dress flapping on my knees like a sheet billowing
in wind, the black earth hinting green under my feet.

I did it even though I loved him. Held my brother
the day he was born, kept him safe from other boys
and their sun-brown hands. We climbed high in the hay,
him and me, stuck our faces out the window
where we could watch the world bending under sky.

I loved his hands that never grew hard, the soft pink flesh,
his silent ways that brought the wild things to him.
Nights I'd reach across our narrow room to stroke his skin,
said I'd marry him if I could.
We stood in the window in the barn. I told him I was Jesus.
If he had faith enough, he'd fly.

The swallows dipped and rose in the air;
the moon, I knew, was God watching what I'd done.
I told him I was Jesus.

Later on I let the older boys touch me with their hands,
my brother on his cot, waiting for me to slip back
through our window, tell him everything they had done,
as if my words to him could fix his bones
mended every way but right.

He shoulda known. *Dammit, he shoulda known.*
A girl can't be Jesus.

And you? If you'd been out walking that day or driving by,
what would you have seen among the black dirt turning green,
except a girl running from a barn, a girl nowhere near Jesus,
her hair flying out behind, mouth open,
a room, a darkness, vast, inside.

Deep Cove

Here the trees close the sky in
while God, who has finished directing
the seasons, curls up to sleep
among horses. God, who is more at home
with the humble. Sleeping in their stalls,
dreaming the depths of their hearts.
The forest after rain, morning, and sky
between the tallest branches a sea
the birds swim in all day, owls sing in
through the night. I keep thinking
if I walk on through this day
and the next and the one after that,
the silence will break. We will speak again.
Stretch out my fingers and touch
the other who is myself.
My heart stayed open the whole time.
No armour. No fence. No padlocks on the gate.
And each morning the horses pass through,
and God banks his fire at the end of the day.

Aubade

We scattered his ashes from the bridge into a northern river, the rapids below, as logging trucks pounded the bridge, the sun fierce, brief. Weeks before, we'd sat together as I read a poem aloud about a man, a death, the words caught in my mouth, something in me sudden, that knew he was about to go. This I could do: the ceremony, the bridge, the ashes wind-gleaned, eddied into the trees, fallen fallow, carried off on the river. But you, you are not the one who died. You, alive, and will not see me. I listen to air and what stories the small birds tell. The remainder of last night's rain clings to barbed wire, the lichened branch, turns the world upside down. The weight of this world that longs for a sleep deaf and blind beneath the snow. But you are alive, and will not, will not. At this bend in the year we burn the deadfall in rain as ravens hurl their arguments on the wind. Each day I play the piano, its long black body a bird caged behind high windows; I brave Bach's unresolved questions, Beethoven's insistence. My invitation to you to hear me play yet unanswered. I set my hands to the keys, the music rising for no one, for me alone, for the few who walk by on the quiet road. I know that music heals, repairs in ways that words have not. You alive, and I afraid of your death. Nights I dream a river between us. The sound of wings in the night. And wonder how far the music can fly.

Rupture

Pearls in a silver
bowl, half
the clasp, no string.

Among the smaller
stars, fallen
planets.

I was your final dance.
The night and its prophets,
all your eyes watching.

You were a road,
a river; now
you're spindrift,
washed up.

Where everything,
eventually, is finished.
Boarded up. Abandoned.
Your cities of ruin.

Little cave
of skulls,
all the names for loss.

Ancient lost tongues.
The hundred hearts
pulsing inside the heart.

Thread by thread.
That's how the world
splits open,
until even the moon
stops eating.

Little runes,
small irritations,
read to me the future's
palm.

You'd think
we could mend,
could hold
each other, gently.
You'd think.

NOTES

"Portrait of the artist with Yu Xuanji (840–868)": Yu Xuanji was a Chinese poet of the late Tang Dynasty. Little is known of her life, yet her poems are distinctive in that she wrote in an autobiographical style instead of using a persona, as was customary at the time. She was put to death at the age of twenty-eight. Her volume of complete poems, *The Clouds Float North*, is published by Wesleyan University Press.

"Fragment of a letter": Canadian soldier George Lawrence Price (15 December 1892–11 November 1918) was the last soldier to die in the First World War, at two minutes to eleven on 11 November 1918. The poem uses paraphrases from letters written by soldiers E.J. Ruffell, Andrew Bowie and George Littlefair. The letters were collected by composer Zachary Wadsworth for his choral composition *When There is Peace*, presented on the CBC program Choral Concert on 11 November 2018. To listen: cbcmusic.ca/programs/choralconcert.

"Mrs. Einstein": For more information on Mileva Einstein's contribution to physics, see "The Forgotten Life of Einstein's First Wife," at blogs.scientificamerican.com.

"Still-life": Over 15 years, while working in secret, the American painter Andrew Wyeth produced a series of more than 240 paintings and live drawings of Helga, a woman who worked as a housekeeper on a nearby farm near Chadds Ford, Pennsylvania. He did so without the knowledge of his wife or the neighbour for whom Helga worked. See "BBC Michael Palin in Wyeth's World," on youtube.com.

"Robert Schumann": Robert Schumann (1810–1856) was a German Romantic composer whose symphonies, piano, and choral works are frequently performed today. Schumann was married to the composer and concert pianist Clara Wiek, and it was she who ultimately placed

Schumann in an asylum, apparently due to bipolar disorder, where he died at the age of forty-six.

"Easter Sunday": The painting is a water colour work in which Helga is the subject.

"Something completely understood, but unspeakable": This is a line taken from "Three Cows and the Moon" by Brigit Pegeen Kelly.

"Getting through the war": The Contras were the various U.S.-backed rebel groups that were active from 1979 to the early 1990s in opposition to the Sandinista government in Nicaragua. During that time, the Contras committed a number of human rights violations, carrying out more than 1,300 attacks. See Gary LaFree, Laura Dugan and Erin Miller, *Putting Terrorism into Context* (Routledge, 2014, p. 56). Witness for Peace, founded in 1983 with the purpose of establishing an ongoing presence in Nicaragua during the Contra war, sent U.S. citizens to accompany the Nicaraguan people living in war zones. It is widely credited with pioneering this tactic of international protective accompaniment (witnessforpeace.org).

"Entreaty": Ludovico Einaudi, born 23 November 1955, is an Italian pianist and composer whose work crosses the boundaries between classical and popular music. His composition, "Elegy for the Arctic," in which he plays a grand piano while drifting on an ice floe, can be viewed on youtube.com.

"Perspective": The phrase *pale blue dot* was coined by the astrophysicist Carl Sagan, when commenting on a photograph of Earth taken by the Voyager 1 spacecraft on 14 February 1990. See "Carl Sagan's Press Release for Voyager's Capture of our pale blue dot" on youtube.com.

"Shepherds": The poem is a response to T.S. Eliot's poem, "The Magi."

ABOUT THE AUTHOR

Patrick Lane has called Pamela Porter "a poet to be grateful for." Her work has earned many accolades, including the inaugural Gwendolyn MacEwan Poetry Prize, the *Malahat Review*'s 50th Anniversary Poetry Prize, the *Our Times* Poetry Award for political poetry, the *FreeFall* Magazine Poetry Award, the *Prism International* Grand Prize in Poetry, the *Vallum* Magazine Poem of the Year Award, as well as the Raymond Souster and Pat Lowther Award shortlists. Her novel in verse, *The Crazy Man,* won the Governor General's Award, the Canadian Library Association Book of the Year for Children Award, the TD Canadian Children's Literature Award and other prizes. Both *The Crazy Man* and her later novel, *I'll Be Watching,* are required reading in schools and colleges across Canada and the U.S. Pamela lives on a farm near Sidney, B.C., with her family and a menagerie of rescued horses, dogs and cats.